The Mickey Mouse Mouse

BOOK CLUB EDITION

Copyright © 1978 by Walt Disney Productions. All rights reserved under International and Pan-American Copyright Conventions. Published in the United States by Random House, Inc., New York, and simultaneously in Canada by Random House of Canada Limited, Toronto.

Library of Congress Cataloging in Publication Data

The Mickey Mouse birthday book.

(Disney's wonderful world of reading, #44)

Minnie gives Mickey a surprise party and the reader learns how she handled invitations, place cards, food, and games.

1. Children's parties—Juvenile literature. 2. Birthdays—Juvenile literature. [1. Parties. 2. Birthdays]   GV1205.M52
793.2'1   78-55911   ISBN 0-394-83963-3   ISBN 0-394-93963-8 (lib. bdg.)

Manufactured in the United States of America 1 2 3 4 5 6 7 8 9 0
A   B   C   D   E   F   G   H   I   J   K

BIRTHDAY BOOK

Random House New York

Mickey woke up early.

He was very happy, because today
was his birthday.

The sun was shining.

"What a beautiful day!" said Mickey.

Mickey washed his face and brushed his teeth.

He put on his new yellow shirt.

He was sure his friends would come over
to wish him a happy birthday.

So he wanted to look nice.

Since it was a special day, Mickey decided
to cook himself a special breakfast.

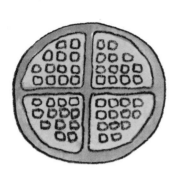

First he made waffles
in the waffle iron.

Next he fried
three pieces of
bacon in the
frying pan.

Then he poured himself
a glass of orange juice.

When the waffles
and bacon were done,
he sat down to eat.

His special breakfast
was so good!

After breakfast he sat in his big chair and read the paper.

He knew that someone would be coming to visit him any minute.

But no one knocked at the door.

And no one called on the telephone.

He looked at the clock.

An hour passed, and nothing happened.

Finally he called up Minnie.
"Do you know what day
it is?" he asked.

"Yes," said Minnie, "it's
Wednesday."
Minnie smiled. She knew
very well that today was
Mickey's birthday.
She was planning
a surprise party for him.

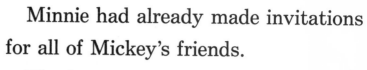

Minnie had already made invitations for all of Mickey's friends.

The invitations were easy to make.

If you want to have a Mickey Mouse birthday party, you can make these invitations, too.

Minnie's Invitations

You will need:

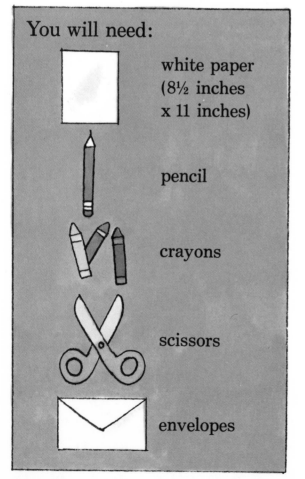

white paper (8½ inches x 11 inches)

pencil

crayons

scissors

envelopes

1 Take one piece of the white paper.

You can make two invitations from each piece.

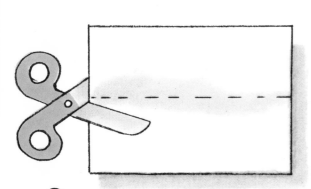

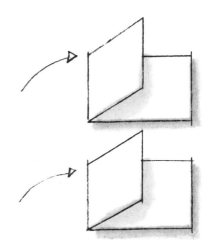

2 Cut the paper in half the long way.

3 Fold each piece in half.

4 Trace or copy this drawing of Mickey on the front of the card.

Color Mickey in. Use your favorite colors for his shirt and pants.

5 Inside the card write the words you see below. Then fill in the blanks.

Then write:

> I'm having a birthday party.
> Day: .... Date: ....
> Time: from .... o'clock
>   to .... o'clock
> ....(your name)......
> ....(address).......
> ....(telephone number).......
>   R.S.V.P.

6 Put each invitation into an envelope.

You can buy envelopes that are the right size.

Or you can make one from another piece of paper.

TAPE

TAPE

If you do make your own envelopes,

put the invitation in the center.

Fold the paper around the invitation.

Tape it closed.

Now you are ready to address and mail it.

After Minnie finished
making the invitations,
she put them
in a mailbox.

So many people!
Where would they all sit?
Minnie made place cards.
Each card had a name on it.

The place cards would tell each of Mickey's friends
where to sit at the table.

What is a little girl after she
is 7 years old?

8 years old

Place cards would be good for your Mickey Mouse party, too.

Want to know how to make them?

Minnie's Lollipop Place Cards

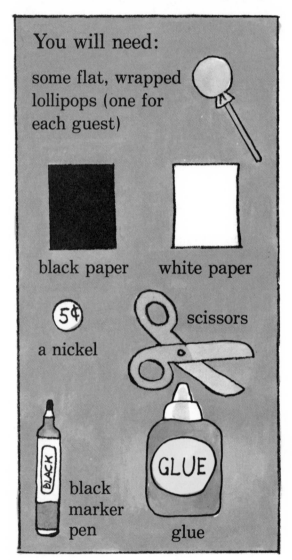

You will need:

some flat, wrapped lollipops (one for each guest)

black paper   white paper

5¢ a nickel

scissors

black marker pen

GLUE glue

1 Make circles on the black paper by drawing around the nickel.

These circles will be mouse ears.

2 Cut out enough circles so you will have two ears for each lollipop.

3 Glue two circles to each lollipop.

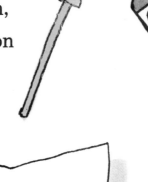

4 With the black marker pen, draw a mouse face like this on the lollipop wrapper.

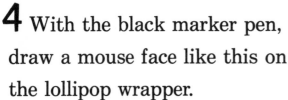

5 Trace this bow onto the sheet of white paper. You will need one bow for each lollipop.

6 Cut out all the bows.

7 Write one guest's name
on each bow.

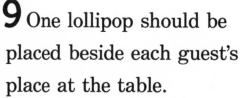

8 Glue one bow on each lollipop.

9 One lollipop should be
placed beside each guest's
place at the table.
Now your friends will
know where to sit.

Goofy wanted to help with the party, too.

So he made goody bags for everyone.

Goody bags are useful for carrying goodies—candy or prizes—home from the party. They are very easy to make. But start working on them at least a week before your own party.

Goofy's Goody Bags

You will need: brown lunch bags (one for each guest)

glue

GLUE

black marker pen

old Mickey Mouse comic books

scissors

1 If you have old comic books, cut out lots of Disney characters.

If you don't, you can trace them from this book.

2 Glue two or three characters on each bag.

3 With the marker pen, draw a "balloon" coming from the mouth of one of the characters.

Have him say: "This goody bag belongs to _____" and fill in the guest's name.

Goofy and Minnie decided to give the bags out at the beginning of the party, as a special surprise.

If you want to make a hole in a brown paper bag, on which side should you make it?

Both sides—inside and outside.

While his friends were
working hard on his party, Mickey
just sat in his chair feeling
more and more unhappy.

Finally he decided to do some
work and forget about his
birthday.

He washed all the
windows in his house.

It took a long time,
but it didn't make him feel
much better.

As he was finishing the
last window, the telephone
rang.

Mickey rushed to pick it up.
Minnie was calling him.

"Mickey," she said, "I would
like to borrow your lawn mower.
Will you please bring it over?"

"Yes," said Mickey. "I'll be
there in a minute."

When Mickey got to Minnie's house, all his friends
stood in the doorway.

"Surprise! Happy birthday!" they shouted.

"Come in and open your presents," said Minnie.
"But leave the lawn mower outside."

Everyone laughed.

Mickey was so happy!

After Mickey opened his presents, Minnie took everyone into the dining room.

It looked beautiful.

Balloons and streamers were hanging from the ceiling.

The table was set, and there was a birthday cake in the center.

Everyone sat down in front of the right place card.

"What a wonderful birthday!" said Mickey.

Minnie served these Crazy Pluto Dogs for lunch.

You can make them for your party, too.

Crazy Pluto Dogs

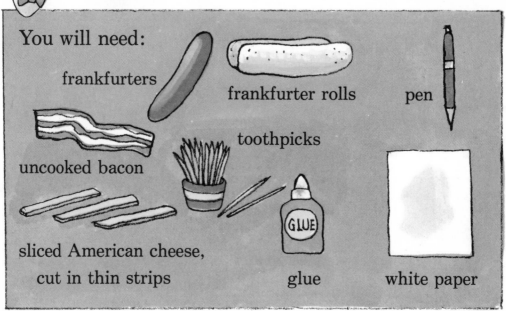

You will need:

frankfurters

frankfurter rolls

pen

uncooked bacon

toothpicks

sliced American cheese, cut in thin strips

glue

white paper

The day before the party:

1 Cut strips of white paper 2 inches long and ½-inch wide.

2 Write something funny on each strip.

3 Glue one strip on each toothpick.

YOU LUCKY DOG

I DON'T BITE BACK

WHAT'S YOUR BEEF

BOW WOW

The day of the party:

1 Cut halfway through each frankfurter, lengthwise.

2 Put strips of cheese in the opening.

3 Wrap a piece of bacon around the frankfurter, from one end to the other.

4 Have a grownup broil the frankfurters until the bacon is brown and crisp.

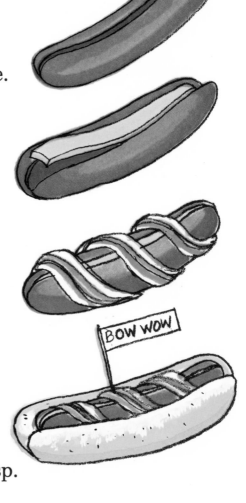

BOW WOW

After each frankfurter has been put in a roll, put one of the funny sayings on the top and serve.

Mickey: What did one hot dog say to the other hot dog?

Minnie: Hi, Frank!

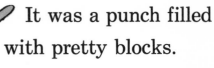

Donald had brought a very special drink for the party.

It was a punch filled with pretty blocks.

The blocks were colored ice cubes.

Anyone can make this wonderful drink.

And it doesn't even have to be for a birthday party.

Donald Duck's Party Punch

Colored Ice Cubes

You will need:

1 package of instant soft drink mix (any flavor)

1 cup sugar (if mix is sugarless)

1 quart water

The day before the party:

1 Stir the soft drink mix and sugar into the water.

2 Pour into ice cube trays and freeze.

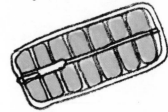

Party Punch (NOTE: Make right before serving)

Makes enough for 12–14 glasses

You will need:

4 cans (6 oz. each) frozen pink lemonade

water

1 quart ginger ale

a punch bowl and cups

1 Mix the lemonade with water as directed on the can.

2 Add the ginger ale.

3 Add the colored ice cubes and serve.

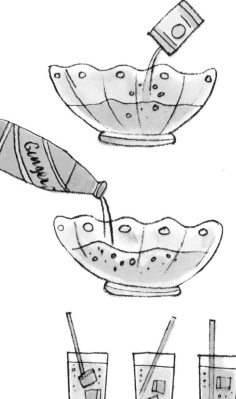

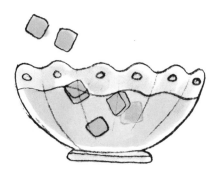

After lunch, Louie came up for another glass of punch. "This is the fourth time you've come back for more punch," said Huey. "Aren't you embarrassed?"

"No!" said Louie. "I keep telling them it's for you."

Later Mickey and his friends played five different games. They had lots of fun. You can have fun playing the games, too.

The first game they played was:

Tape the Flowers on Mickey

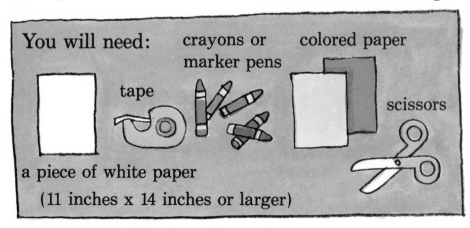

You will need: crayons or   colored paper
                  marker pens

tape

scissors

a piece of white paper
    (11 inches x 14 inches or larger)

Get ready for the game before your party:

1 Draw Mickey on the white paper.

You can use this picture as a guide.

But you will have to draw Mickey almost as big as the sheet of paper.

2 Cut flowers like these from the colored paper.

You will need one flower for each person at the party. Cut a piece of tape for each flower.

To play the game:

1 Hang the drawing of Mickey on the wall.

2 Give each person a flower with a piece of tape on it.

3 One at a time, have each person close his eyes and try to tape the flower on Mickey's hand.

At the end of the game, the person whose flower is closest to Mickey's hand is the winner.

When the clock strikes 13 at a party, what time is it?   Time to get the clock fixed

Uncle Scrooge's Penny Game

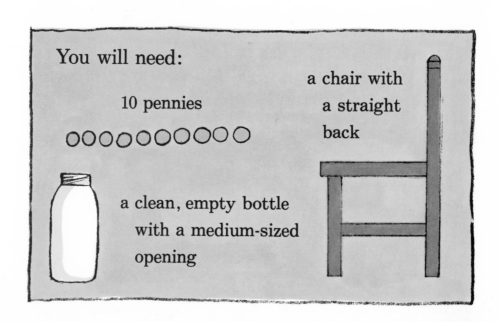

You will need:

10 pennies

a chair with
a straight
back

a clean, empty bottle
with a medium-sized
opening

1 Put the bottle on the floor in back of the chair.

2 One at a time, have each person kneel on the chair and reach over the back.

3 Give each person 10 pennies.

4 He or she must then try to drop the pennies one by one into the bottle.

5 The person who is able to put the most pennies in the bottle is the winner and gets to keep the pennies as a prize.

What did one penny say to another penny?

Together we make more cents

Huey, Louie and Dewey's:
Duck Walk Relay Race

You will need:

one chair for each team

1 Divide people into two teams.

Each team should have the same number of players.

2 Before the race starts, have everyone practice walking like a duck.

Stoop in a deep knee bend.

Place hands on hips (like wings).

Waddle forward.

3 Line up each team, one member behind the other. Give the signal to start.

The first person in each line waddles around the chair and returns, touching the next person in line.

4 The race continues until everyone has had a turn.

5 The first team to finish wins the race.

Each winning team member gets two special lollipops.

Each losing team member gets one special lollipop for trying so hard.

After the relay race,
Donald walked over to shake
Goofy's hand, because Goofy
was one of the winners.

Goofy took his hands
out of his pockets.

"Goodness, Goofy," said
Donald, "your hands seem
very sticky today."

"Yours would, too," Goofy
answered, "if you had a piece
of birthday cake in each
pocket."

Now it was Daisy's turn to pick a favorite game.

She asked everyone to sit in a circle.

Then she told them how to play.

You can have fun with this game at your own party.

Daisy's Telephone Mix-Up Game

Before the party, make up several sentences and write them on different pieces of paper.

An example might be: "Mabel's great-grandmother went to the store and bought a pink cotton dress with lace."

1 Seat everyone in a circle.

2 Give one person a sentence and have him whisper it into the ear of the person sitting on his left side.

3 Each player, in turn, should continue to whisper the sentence until the last person in the circle hears it.

He then says it out loud so
everyone can hear.

4 The first person should then read the
message on the paper.
Usually there is quite a difference!

5 Now give a new sentence to a different
person.
It should be whispered from person to
person the way the first sentence was.

6 Continue playing until everyone has
had a chance to start a message
around the circle.

This funny game will show
you and your guests
how easy it is to get
messages mixed up.

Pluto's Buried Bone Game

You will need:

a large bag of hard candies wrapped in paper
These will be Pluto's "bones."

Before the party: Hide the pieces of candy all over
a room where the guests won't be playing.

1 When you are ready to play the game, have your guests get their Goofy Goody Bags or give them other paper bags.

Then take them into the room where the "bones" are hidden.

2 Tell your guests that they will have ten minutes to locate all the "bones" in the room and put them in their bags.

3 At the end of the ten minutes, the one who has found the most "bones" is the winner.

Let the guests take home the candy they have found.

After Mickey's friends had played all these
games, the party was over.

The guests waved good-by as they started off
toward home.

"This is the best birthday I've ever had," said Mickey.
"But this morning I thought you had all forgotten."

"We would never forget your birthday," said Minnie.
"You should know that!"